D1016183

A Gift For:

_____

From:

_____

To ma ma

From Cara

SHORT PRAYERS
for Busy Women

HARRIET CROSBY

Andrews McMeel
Publishing

GIFT BOOKS
from Hallmark

Short Prayers for Busy Women
Originally copyrighted as *God Help Me,* 1999 by Harriet Crosby.

This edition published in 2004 by Andrews McMeel Publishing exclusively
for Hallmark Cards, Inc., Kansas City, MO 64141.

Visit us on the Web at www.Hallmark.com.

ISBN: 0-7407-5121-2

Design by UDG│DesignWorks, Sisters, OR

Printed and bound in China

BOK5111

For George Leis

who likes to see his name in print

Contents

Introduction

I open my day-planner calendar to review today's
schedule. It's going to be a busy Friday: Four
meetings at work this morning, and a project
deadline to meet by two o'clock. Rush home and
take the cats to the vet for their annual vaccinations.
Straighten up the house. Make dinner for four
people and entertain them throughout the evening.
And I see Saturday isn't much better—in addition
to spending time with various friends and family,
I've got a list of errands and chores to do that's
longer than my arm.

Martha is a terrific Christian. She does everything right. She welcomes Jesus into her home and offers him hospitality to make him comfortable. Who can blame her if she gets just a bit frazzled, what with doing this and that with no help at all? Meanwhile, Martha's sister, Mary, sits all dreamy-eyed, resting at Jesus' feet, doing nothing but hanging on his every word. Jesus seems to be enjoying himself immensely. So Martha takes a small shot at Mary through Jesus: "Lord, do you not care that my sister has left me to do all the work by myself? Tell her then to help me." Lord, do you not care…? Martha's shot hit the bull's-eye, and Jesus feels the sting of her words. With boundless tenderness he looks straight into Martha's anxious heart. After a long silence, Jesus almost whispers, "Martha, Martha, you are worried and distracted by many things: there is need of only one thing. Mary has chosen the better part, which will not be taken away from her."

Mary is a mystic. She chose "the better part," to sit quietly at Jesus' feet, gaze on him, and contemplate his words. She is quiet. Rarely does Mary say a word. I've always imagined Mary as a woman who led a lively spiritual life on the inside, invisible to all but God.

Martha's spiritual life is lived very much on the outside. She follows the ancient Jewish practice of hospitality. She is outspoken, telling Jesus exactly what's on her mind. She is pragmatic and down-to-earth (later, at the death of her brother Lazarus, Martha cautions Jesus against the stench that surely fills the tomb). Notice that Jesus does not condemn Martha or her hospitable efforts. Martha isn't doing anything wrong. She is in no way inferior to her sister, Mary. Jesus simply points out that only "one thing" is needed—to listen to his words.

Most of us are full-time Marthas and part-time Marys. While there are certainly some rare times

of rest and contemplation in our lives, most of us
are called to be busy women like Martha. We have
jobs to do, families to raise, church or community
responsibilities. God calls us to these things as
surely as Mary was called to sit at Jesus' feet.
And yet, busy Marthas that we are, we each feel
the stirrings of Mary inside us too. It's no accident
that these very different women are related by
blood. As sisters, each complements the other.
Jesus enjoys the friendship of both. They represent
two sides of the spiritual life: a life devoted to God
in the world and a life devoted to God in the heart.

Again I look at my calendar. I envy Mary. But I
celebrate Martha because God is calling me to this
life, to my life, which is full-time and busy—and
belongs to God. This book is for women like me,
full-time Marthas and part-time Marys. The prayers
in this book are for busy women whose hearts
belong to God.

These prayers celebrate Martha while honoring Mary in each of us. In the midst of our busy days, we can let ourselves be Mary and hang on God's every word in prayer. But these prayers aren't reserved for quiet moments or times of serenity and inner peace. Sometimes our really heartfelt prayers are prayed when we are most overwhelmed, coping with some kind of crisis, or so busy we're just barely hanging in there. These prayers are to be prayed when we are right in the thick of our days and need a few words to give us the strength to do the next thing.

Short Prayers for Busy Women is designed to be carried with you in a briefcase or purse. It contains small prayers on a variety of topics to use throughout the day. These brief words let the Mary in you strengthen the Martha. Say them whenever and wherever you choose, alone or with others. There is need of only one thing on this busy day—pray.

Short Prayers for Busy Women

Hours & Days

God,

There is never enough time.

Help me to make wise decisions

about how to spend it.

Guide me to use my time for

those things—and people—

that are most important to me.

Amen

Schedules

God,

I love you.

Never forget that I love you.

No matter how busy I am,

I love you.

I thought you should know.

Amen

God,

I need to spend time with you.

Help me to make sure there's room

for you in my schedule.

Amen

Schedules

Hours & Days

God,
I just can't do everything.
Show me what I can do.
Show me what I need to let go of
and give me the courage
to walk away.
Amen

God,

My schedule is more than

just a list of appointments.

My schedule shows me what and

who is important to me.

Help me to organize my priorities.

Amen

Schedules

God,

This morning is

so beautiful and still.

I hear the whisper

of your voice in the silence.

I'm glad you're here

with me now.

Amen

God,

There is not enough time
in the morning. I have to get
everybody else ready and out the door
before I can get myself ready to go too.
Help me to remember to talk
with you first thing
every morning.
Amen

Mornings

God,

This morning promises a new day

filled with new beginnings.

Help me not to waste

any opportunities to start fresh.

Open my eyes to see

open doors today.

Amen

God,

I want to crawl back into bed.

I just can't face another day.

Give me the strength I need to work

and to love.

Walk with me and let me know

that I don't go forth into this day alone.

Amen

Mornings

Hours & Days

God,
The day is half over.
Thank you for all
I've been able to accomplish.
Give me the energy I need
to finish the day well.
Amen

God,

I'm too busy today to

take time for lunch.

But I am aware of your presence

even now.

Thank you for standing by me

in this zoo.

Amen

Hours & Days

God,

Thank you for this chance

to take a break in the afternoon.

I can catch my breath

and tell you that I love you.

I love you.

Amen

Afternoons

God,

Today has been such a gift.

I pause this afternoon

to give you thanks for work to do

and people to love—

and for the beauty of this day.

Amen

God,

The sun is setting

and at last I can look toward home.

As this day ends and work ceases,

help me to know that it's you

I come home to.

Amen

God,

I may be on my way home

from work now,

but my second job is about to begin.

Help me to get dinner,

give baths, make conversation,

listen to my family.

And after all these things are done,

help me to get a little rest.

Amen

God,

The evening is so peaceful and quiet.

There's a very faint glow

in the sky where the sun used to be.

As the morning is your creation,

so is the evening.

All praise to you.

Amen

God,

Thank you for the day

that has passed.

Help me find you in the night

that is to come.

And when we meet,

let me know the power

of your love.

Amen

Evenings

God,

Finally a little space and quiet.

The house is still.

I hear only the sound of my own breath.

Thank you for the quiet

of this night and for your presence

in the darkness.

Amen

God,

Protect all who live

within this house from the fears

and dangers of the night.

Let your presence shine quietly

in the dark.

Bring us in safety to

a new day filled with the

hope of your love.

Amen

Nights

God,

Help me to get some sleep!

I'm so anxious and wound up

that I can't keep my eyes closed.

Relieve my worried mind.

Help me to rest in you.

Amen

God,

I don't spend enough time
looking at the stars. Looking
at the stars tonight reminds
me that the most important
thing in the universe is love—
love of you, of family, of friends.
Help me never to take love for granted.

Amen

Hours & Days

God,
I look at the week ahead
and wonder how
I'm going to get through it.
Help me not to anticipate the days
that lie ahead but to live each one,
knowing that you walk
with me in the future.
Amen

God,

What a week!

The weekend is coming, and

I badly need a little rest and recreation.

Help me to recover from these five

busy, tumultuous days.

Help me have a little fun.

Amen

Hours & Days

God,

How I wish I could live my life

on my own time instead of living the

days around the work week

and the school week.

But work and school are here

to stay for now.

Help me to find time for myself

in a week largely outside of my control.

Amen

Weeks

40

God,

Another month gone.

The season is beginning to change.

Help me to accept the joys

and challenges of the coming month

with grace and peace.

Amen

Hours & Days

God,

I just turned the page in my calendar.

What happened to next month?

There's too much to do

in too little time.

Help me not to waste the coming days.

Help me to savor each one

in spite of the busyness.

Amen

Months

God,

This month looks like it's going

to be a quiet one.

Keep me from filling up

every day with busyness.

Help me to

leave plenty of time

for doing nothing at all.

Amen

God,
The thought of next year
overwhelms me.
All the birthdays and anniversaries,
annual checkups and reviews,
all the triumphs and all the losses
yet to be lived. Help me to live each day
one at a time, relying on your love
to take care of me.
Amen

Years

44

Hours & Days

God,

Another year is gone.

Am I any wiser? Maybe a little.

One thing I know for sure:

You walked with me through every hour

of every day, though I could not always

feel your presence.

Thank you for what has passed,

and thank you for what is to come.

Amen

Short Prayers for Busy Women

Family & Friends

Family & Friends

God,

Take care of my children

while I am away from them today.

Keep them safe;

let them know you are near.

And help me

not to worry about them.

Amen

Kids

Family & Friends

God,
There are too many noisy kids
in this car pool,
and I think I'm going to scream.
Form in me a place
that's quiet and let me
walk with you there,
away from car pools and
traffic and kids.
Amen

Kids

Family & Friends

God,

Are you sure children are a blessing?

All the worry,

late nights, expense.

But I've never loved like this before;

they are more precious to me

than life itself.

Thank you, God,

for my children.

Amen

Kids

God,

My kids are turning into people!

I wish I could go

with them everywhere

and protect them from all

the bad things that can happen in life.

But I can't. Give me the love

I need to let them go

and make their own way.

Amen

Kids

Family & Friends

God,

The kids wanted dinner

an hour ago,

and I just got home.

They're wild.

You know what kind

of day I've had.

Give me the strength

to provide for them

as you provide for me.

Amen

Kids

Family & Friends

God,

He can be a pain!

But at least he's my pain.

Help me to love him

in spite of all the annoying

little things he does.

Because I do love him, and I

want to love him more.

Amen

Family & Friends

God,

Men. Who needs them?

I do. I don't like being alone

just now and could use

some male companionship.

Would you please send

a little my way?

Amen

Spouse / Partner

Family & Friends

God,
I didn't know I could
love someone so much.
I didn't know someone could
love me so much.
Keep us in love,
O God, and guard our love
through thick and thin.
Amen

Spouse / Partner

Family & Friends

God,
We're going through
a tough time right now.
We're traveling blind
through a strange country.
Help us both to find our way.
And let us find you
at the end of our journey.
Amen

Spouse / Partner

Family & Friends

God,

It's just another ordinary day.

But I am so grateful,

O God, for my helper,

friend, and lover.

Never let me

take him for granted.

Amen

Family & Friends

God,
You know my parents
drive me crazy.
Be with me while I'm with them.
Grant me the serenity
I need to honor them.
Amen

Parents

Family & Friends

God,
I still love my parents
with a child's love.
I know you love them
even more than I do.
Take care of them and
keep them in the palm
of your hand.
Amen

Parents

Family & Friends

God,
Show me how to
love my parents today.
Help me to be
my best with them.
And keep me from
taking them for granted.
Amen

Parents

Family & Friends

God,

I miss my parents

and wish they were here.

Keep me company

in their absence and help me

to remember that

you are my heavenly parent.

Amen

Parents

Family & Friends

God,
Help me in my role
as daughter-in-law.
Guide me and direct me
in my relationship
with my in-laws,
and help me to see
the light of your love
in their eyes.
Amen

In-Laws

Family & Friends

God,

Give me strength.

It's time for the in-laws.

Help me to deal with them

with dignity and respect.

Amen

Family & Friends

God,

Thank you for my in-laws,

for their love and care.

I couldn't ask for better parents.

I'm glad they are family.

Amen

In-Laws

Family & Friends

God,

Thank you for my family.

Loving them isn't always easy.

But sometimes,

when I look in their eyes,

I see you looking out at me,

and I tremble

with love for them.

Thank you.

Amen

Family

Family & Friends

God,

Thank you for friends.

I can trust in your goodness

and mercy because

you've brought them into my life.

Bless our friendship

and help it to

grow and deepen.

Amen

Friends

Family & Friends

God,

I could use

a few friends right now.

Everything feels

strange and uncertain.

Friendship is

such a great anchor.

Please send a friend my way.

Amen

Friends

Family & Friends

God,

Help me to be the kind of friend
I would want to have.
Strengthen my loyalty in the
relationship through
fair weather and foul.
And let us always find
joy and delight in each other.
Amen

Friends

Family & Friends

God,
Sometimes when
the going gets tough,
a few good friends
are hard to find.
Show me who my real friends are.
Let me lean on the
strength of their love.
Amen

Family & Friends

God,
It's so hard to say good-bye!
Help us find a way
to maintain our friendship
across the
miles that separate us.
Amen

Family & Friends

God,

My pet may not be human,

but he is a true friend.

Thank you, God,

for such a faithful,

loyal companion.

I love him very much.

Amen

Pets

Family & Friends

God,

You are the Creator

of all creatures, great and small.

Keep my furry friend

in good health.

May she always

be playful and happy,

get plenty to eat, and have

lots of naps in the sun.

Amen

Pets

Family & Friends

God,

my beloved pet is sick.

Let him know your healing touch.

Hold him in the palm

of your hand.

Help me to make

the best decisions I can

about his care.

Amen

Pets

Short Prayers for Busy Women

Peace & Serenity

Peace & Serenity

God,

It's easy to love my family and friends
when times are good
and things are going well.
Help me to love them when the going
gets tough–like right now.
Teach me to love them
as you love them: freely, expecting
nothing in return.

Amen

Unconditional Love

Peace & Serenity

God,

There's someone

I don't love much right now.

But I want to be loving in spite

of my feelings.

Give me the courage

and grace to love even though

I don't feel like it.

Amen

Unconditional Love

Peace & Serenity

God,
I don't know why you love me–
but you do.
Your love for me
is a complete mystery.
Help me give up trying to understand
or rationalize your love;
help me to accept
it as a fabulous gift.
Amen

Unconditional Love

Peace & Serenity

God,

Thank you for this life,

for all you've given me to do,

for all the people who

both love and challenge me.

I know you speak to me in this life

in every moment of every day.

Give me ears

to hear your voice.

Amen

Gratitude

Peace & Serenity

God,

Simple kindness

doesn't get a lot of press these days,

but I sure could use

a little right now.

Show me some kindness today.

And help me to pass

a little of your kindness

along to someone else.

Amen

Kindness

Peace & Serenity

God,
I'm sick and tired
of beating myself up.
I wouldn't treat my dog
the way I treat myself.
Help me to show
some kindness to myself today.
Help me to lighten up—
and let in your love.
Amen

Kindness

God,

Strangers scare me.

But I know that not all strangers

want to hurt me.

Help me be a little kinder

to people I don't know—

for I may someday be kind

to an angel in disguise.

Amen

Kindness

Peace & Serenity

God,

Help me to be faithful to

the people who matter most—

my family and friends.

Let me show them

that they can depend on me

for love no matter what.

Help my love to be like yours,

solid and unchanging.

Amen

Faithfulness

God,
Your faithfulness to me
is beyond measure.
I look back over my life
and cannot count how many times
your hand has been upon me
to provide for me,
strengthen me, love me.
To you I give all my thanks.
Amen

Faithfulness

God,

This is a faithless world.

Loyalties and allegiances change

and shift from moment to moment.

Love that was here yesterday

is gone tomorrow. But you,

O God, are my rock; your faithfulness

toward me is unchanging. Help me to

lean on your faithfulness now.

Amen

Faithfulness

Peace & Serenity

God,

There is so much going on today

that I've lost sight of you.

But I know even now

you shadow my every step.

Give me the strength I need to trust

that you are with me even though the

clamor of events and people may

seem to keep you away.

Amen

Faithfulness

Peace & Serenity

God,
You promise me peace.
I believe you can
deliver on your promise.
Help me to find something
of your peace today.
Amen

Peace

Peace & Serenity

God,
I am not
a naturally calm person.
I need your help.
Help me to rest–if only
for a few minutes today–
in your peace.
Amen

Peace & Serenity

God,
I'm asking for a miracle.
When friends, colleagues, and
family see me today,
let them see your peace in me.
For I know that
peacemakers are blessed.
Amen

Peace

Peace & Serenity

God,
Help me to be generous
with more than just my money.
Give to me a generous spirit.
Help me to give myself
away more often.
Amen

Generosity

Peace & Serenity

God,
I know you are pleased
with a generous spirit.
Help me to
be generous with love
and acceptance—
of myself and others.
Amen

Generosity

Peace & Serenity

God,

Help me to know

that there is enough

and more than enough

of your love to go around.

Let me be generous

with your love toward

whomever I meet today.

Amen

Generosity

Short Prayers for Busy Women

Career & Work

God,
I hear you calling
me for something special.
Give me the
patience and strength
to follow my vocation.
Guide my footsteps to
become the one you are
calling me to be.
Amen

Vocation

God,
I thank you that
my job is my vocation.
For this blessing,
I am truly grateful.
I am grateful that your hand
is upon me,
and that you give me the grace
to do my work with joy.
Amen

Vocation

God,
I may not get paid for it,
but you've given me a passion
for my hobby.
For the joy it brings to me and others,
I am very grateful.
Help me to grow and flourish
in my craft, that I may
always delight in it.
Amen

Avocation

God,
The time I can spend
working on my pastime
is holy time.
Let me always know
that to work at this
is to worship you.
For this sacred time
I offer thanks.
Amen

Avocation

God,

All work,

when dedicated and

offered to you, is holy.

It might be just a job—

but I dedicate it to you,

that I may find you today at work.

I offer my job to you,

that I may work your will.

Amen

Job

God,

I hate my job.

But I need it.

See me through today,

and keep me from

doing something I'll regret.

Help me come another step closer

to finding other work

that better suits me.

Amen

Job

God,

I love my job.

Thank you for this rare blessing.

In a world where

too many people's work

is drudgery,

let me never take my job

for granted.

Amen

Job

Career & Work

God,
It's Monday and
I hope I've won the lottery.
But I doubt it.
Give me the motivation,
strength, patience, and wisdom
I need to do a good job,
today and
throughout the week.
Amen

Job

104

God,

I know life isn't fair.

But sometimes life at work

really isn't fair.

Give me the strength to

change the things I can

and the wisdom to accept

what I can't change.

And guide me with your Spirit.

Amen

Job

God,
Just because I'm retired
doesn't mean I don't work.
No matter how large
or small the tasks today,
help me to do them well.
And let me have
fun while I'm at it.
Amen

God,
Retirement isn't all
it's cracked up to be.
Give me the blessing
of doing something meaningful
with the rest of my life.
Let me enjoy you and this time
we have together.
Amen

Retirement

Career & Work

God,

Today is holy.

I give you thanks for this day.

Keep me from

taking it for granted.

Let all I do today

show forth your glory.

Amen

Retirement

God,

I need a job.

Help me find one.

And until I find one,

give me all I need

to live and thrive.

Amen

Unemployment

God,

What am I going to do now?

Show me what kind

of work you want me to do.

Give me the courage

to explore and learn

as much as I can about

what I am to do for a living.

Amen

Unemployment

Career & Work

God,

Money is tight.

I know money isn't everything—

but it sure means a lot just now.

Help me with my finances.

And provide me with

a job that pays the bills.

Amen

Unemployment

111

God,

I love money.

Keep me from loving it too much.

Give me the courage

and generosity of heart

to give some of it away

to those in need.

Amen

Money

God,

All good gifts

come from you–even money.

Help me to be wise and

generous in its use.

And help me always to

remember that you alone

are the source

of my good fortune.

Amen

Money

God,
Surely a little
more money
than I have right now
couldn't hurt.
Please.
Amen

God,

Help me to be

a good steward of my money.

Help me to invest it wisely

and spend it honorably.

Let there always be

enough to share with my

family and friends and

those in need.

Amen

Money

God,

Open my mind.

Help me to

greet new ideas with joy—

instead of seeing them as

just more things to remember.

May what I learn today

shape me in your image.

Amen

Continuing Education

God,

Work, school,

family, and friends:

There's too much to juggle.

Help me to focus and

concentrate on one thing at a time.

Help me to learn what

I need to learn

in school today.

Amen

Continuing Education

Career & Work

God,
Thank you
for the opportunity to learn.
Help me not to
waste today's opportunity.
Make my mind like a sponge,
absorbing new ideas and
experiences to enrich my life.
Amen

Continuing Education

God,

School is not easy for me.

I need you to help me

through classes today.

Help me to relax in your presence,

knowing that you'll

go to school with me.

Amen

Continuing Education

God,

It is such a privilege

to volunteer.

Help me to do

good work today.

And help the lives

of all those I touch.

Amen

Volunteer Work

God,

I love my work as a volunteer.

Help me to remember that

what I do will benefit

not only those with whom

I come in contact today,

but also people whose names

I'll never know.

Amen

Volunteer Work

Career & Work

God,
This is one of the few times
I can spend alone with you.
Guide my thoughts;
let me rest in your peace;
strengthen my heart
for whatever comes next.
Amen

While Commuting

God,

Thank you for today.

Thank you for the work

you've given me to do.

Help me to do my best

and to remember that,

no matter what I do today,

you hold me

in the palm of your hand.

Amen

While Commuting

God,

As I approach the office,

strengthen me for the day ahead.

Help me to see your

hand at work in all I do.

Help me to see you

in the eyes of my co-workers.

Let this be a good day.

Amen

While Commuting

God,

To say that today stunk

is an understatement.

Today, work was rotten.

But you know that.

Rebuild my spirit as I journey home.

Bless me with a calmness

I do not yet feel.

Amen

While Commuting

God,

Thank you for

the day that is past.

As I turn toward home,

help me to let go.

Help me to leave work thoughts,

worries, and victories at the office.

Clear my mind

to know only your love.

Amen

While Commuting

God,

What an idiot!

Help me with my attitude

toward my boss.

Help me to stop thinking

of him as an idiot

and to see that he is here

to do a job

just like I am.

Amen

Boss

God,

Help me not to
take my boss for granted.
Working for this special person
is a personal as well as
a professional joy.
My boss is a blessing sent by you.
Many thanks.
Amen

BOSS

God,

Help me to see my boss

as you do.

Let me treat my boss

with dignity and respect

so that both of us can get

on with the job.

Amen

Boss

God,
They say American workers like me
are supposed to be competitive.
Help me to compete
in a healthy way.
Keep me from feelings of
professional jealousy or envy
so that together my colleagues
and I can do good work.
Amen

Co-Workers

God,

I have a responsibility

to my staff

to be the best leader and

mentor I can be.

That's a pretty tall order.

I can't do it all alone.

Help me to be

a good, fair boss.

Amen

Staff

God,
There's so much to do today.
I know you will be
at work among us.
Help me to motivate and
lead my staff so we
can all get our work done
on time and within budget.
Amen

Staff

God,
I hate managing people.
One person in particular
has been such a pain.
I know I must bring up some
difficult things.
Help me to be fair, cool,
and clear as we talk.
Amen

Staff

God,

I've got the best staff

in the world.

And I know each and every one

of them is a gift from you.

Thank you, God.

Help me to never

take them for granted.

Amen

Staff

Short Prayers for Busy Women

Body & Health

God,
Look what that scale says!
Something must be done.
Help me to find and
use a diet that helps me
control my weight,
yet doesn't subtract
from my joy in living.
Amen

Weight

God,
Help me to eat
properly and well.
Help me to honor my body
by feeding it healthy food.
Help me to remember
that my body is
a temple.
Amen

Weight

God,
I'm losing weight from stress.
This is not good.
Help me to relax
and find my balance again.
Help me let go of that which
I cannot control
so I can increase
my appetite for living.
Amen

Weight

God,

Too fat. Too thin.

I'm sick and tired of stressing about it!

Help me remember

that you love me

just the way I am.

Let me know

your loving presence

deep in my heart.

Amen

God,
Look at that
great woman in the mirror!
I feel good today.
I'm going to knock 'em dead!
Thank you, God,
for this beautiful feeling.
Amen

God,

Too often I wonder

whether I'm loved for my appearance.

I want to be loved for

who I am inside.

Help me to know that

I am loved for the beauty

of my spirit.

Amen

Beauty

God,

I'm afraid of getting older.

I'm afraid he won't love me anymore.

I'm afraid of one day

losing my job because I am

no longer young.

Help me to trust in your love

and care instead of youth and beauty.

For I know you love me as I am.

Amen

Aging

Body & Health

God,
It's clear that I'm getting older.
Once-firm muscles
are sagging a little.
Help me to
grow old gracefully—
to accept and love
my aging body.
Amen

Aging

God,

I hate getting old.

I hate not being able to do

everything I used to do.

I hate looking in the mirror.

Help me not to

hate growing old anymore.

Help me find a place

of serenity about aging.

Amen

Aging

God,
It's great being an
"older person."
At last I can do what
I want without much concern
about what others think of me.
Help me to use
my freedom wisely,
that I may love and live well.
Amen

Aging

God,

I've been expecting this.

I didn't expect how

big a change it would be, though.

Help me walk through

this time in my life carefully,

one step at a time.

Let me learn to love

the person I am becoming.

Amen

Menopause

Body & Health

God,
Menopause is wild!
I don't know how I'm going to feel
from one minute to the next.
As I journey throughout
this part of my life, help me
to experience your faithfulness.
Let me know that
you never change.
Amen

Menopause

God,
I feel like everybody's looking
at me differently.
Yet I know the real issue is
that I need to look
at myself differently
as I go through menopause.
Help me to love
the person I come to see.
Amen

Menopause

Body & Health

God,
I'm pregnant!
I could burst with joy!
I have no words
to tell you how I feel—
only that
I am so deeply grateful for
the gift of this child.
Amen

God,

I'm pregnant!

This is not supposed to happen.

I'm terrified beyond words.

What am I going to do?

Show me a way.

Amen

Pregnancy

God,
Help this child grow strong
and sound within me.
Surround my baby with your love
as I surround my baby
with my body.
For I know you hold us both
in the palm of your hand.
Amen

God,

Pregnancy is not unending bliss.

I feel rotten.

My ankles are swollen.

I'm enormous—

I have trouble getting up

from the couch. I'm exhausted.

Please let this

baby come soon!

Amen

Pregnancy

God,

Leave me alone!

I hate everybody.

I know my hormones are

on a rampage, but today

I hate the world.

There's nothing you

or I can do.

That's how I feel.

Amen

PMS

God,

The "curse" isn't menstruation,

it's PMS.

Everybody's steering clear of me.

I feel lonely

and a little angry.

Keep me company

for a while.

Amen

PMS

God,

Help me to

manage my emotions

in spite of my hormones today.

Help me to remember

to breathe slowly and deeply

to avoid getting uptight.

Help me to remember that

you love me just as I am.

Amen

PMS

Short Prayers for Busy Women

Home & Garden

God,

My garden makes

my heart sing your praises.

I give you thanks

for the abundant life all around me,

especially my plants.

Let my thanks be as pleasing

to you as birdsong.

Amen

The Garden

Home & Garden

God,

This winter's day,

let my garden sleep in peace.

As it sleeps, help prepare it

for a glorious spring.

And let me dream of new life

during this winter's night.

Amen

The Garden

Home & Garden

God,

Help my garden
grow full and healthy.
Defend it from birds and insects
that would destroy it.
Give me the patience and
diligence I need
to nurture my garden
to beauty and abundance.
Amen

The Garden

Home & Garden

God,
Bless the earth
in which my garden grows.
Bless all the plants and flowers
and vegetables that grow there.
May the rains be gentle and the
sun shine on it warmly.
Amen

The Garden

Home & Garden

God,
It's good to be home.
I hope heaven is like this—
that comforting feeling
of homecoming
after work is through,
to find your welcoming arms
on just the other side
of the front door.
Amen

The Living Room

God,

Bless this room

that holds family and friends.

Let it be a place

of peace and harmony,

a place where we can enjoy

and love one another.

Let it be a place

of comfort and recreation.

Amen

The Living Room

God,

So much living

has been done in this room.

Heal any discord

that has happened here.

Mend any hearts that

have been broken here.

Let your spirit

live here among us.

Amen

The Living Room

God,

May this room

be filled with welcome

from a busy and noisy world.

Let all hearts who enter here

find warmth,

comfort, and healing.

Let all hearts who enter

here find you.

Amen

The Living Room

God,
May all who eat at this table
remember that the
meals served here
come from your hand.
Help us to be always grateful
for our daily bread
and to use it to sustain
our bodies and our minds.
Amen

The Dining Room

God,

Let this room be a place where

we perpetually offer you our thanks.

For all good things, O God,

come from your hand.

Whenever family

and friends enter here,

create in us

grateful and loving hearts.

Amen

The Dining Room

God,

May all who join around this table put

away the cares and troubles of the world

so that we may find you among us.

As we humbly eat of the food

you provide, put away from us

all discord and struggle.

And let us rejoice in each other, in the

food before us, and in your presence.

Amen

The Dining Room

God,
This is the best room.
My kitchen is the heart
of our house.
May it always be warm
and welcoming and
filled with good things.
Amen

The Kitchen

God,

This house is a zoo.

There's so much going on,

running in and out, so much to do.

Help me to be a still point

in my kitchen;

let me know your peace.

Amen

The Kitchen

God,

I don't want to cook tonight.

But others are depending on me.

Give me strength.

Help me figure out something

that's good–and quick.

Amen

The Kitchen

God,

After the day I've had,

going to bed feels so good.

Surely this is the best time of day.

Help my body and mind

relax in your presence

with me this night.

And let me awake in the morning

refreshed and ready to go.

Amen

The Bedroom

God,
This room is not only
a place to rest but also
a place to love.
Help me to be a good lover,
that I may honor and love
my partner with my body
as well as my heart.
Amen

The Bedroom

Home & Garden

God,

It's 2 a.m. and I'm so tense and anxious;

I feel like I'm levitating

three feet above the bed.

Calm my mind; soothe my body.

Help me to relax

into the comfort of the mattress,

the soft warmth of the blankets.

Help me get some sleep.

Amen

The Bedroom

God,

It's so lonely

to be in a bed with someone

when love is gone.

What am I going to do?

Show me a way out.

And for this night,

help me to rest,

somehow, in you.

Amen

The Bedroom

God,

Look at them.

They finally crashed.

They're such angels

when they're asleep.

Bless them and keep them safe

throughout the night

in this room.

Amen

The Kids' Room

God,
What's going on in there?
I don't know which is worse,
too much quiet or
too much noise.
Help me to respect
my children's privacy and yet
intervene when I must.
Amen

The Kids' Room

God,

This is a room in which

my children will make memories.

Let it be filled with

fun and happiness.

Help them to grow up

good and strong.

Amen

The Kids' Room

God,

I love this room the best.

It is a place of my own where

I can read, think,

and take care of my own business.

Help me to grow and

thrive here in all

that I do.

Amen

The Study/Den

God,

I don't care about

using this room to study;

I come here

for peace and quiet.

In this room I can hear myself think.

Help me to hear you

speaking to me as well.

Amen

The Study/Den

God,
My study is filled with books.
Help me to listen carefully
to the writers as I read.
Help me never to lose
that sense of wonder that
their books inspire.
Amen

The Study/Den

God,

When I shut the door to the bathroom,

it becomes the one room in the house

where my family can't follow me.

Let me sit here quietly

for a little while.

Give me the strength and energy

I need to love them

when I come out.

Amen

The Bathroom

God,

This bathtub is my sanctuary.

Help my body to relax

in the warm, fragrant water.

Heal my mind of the

day's problems and traumas.

Let the only voice I hear

be yours.

Amen

The Bathroom

Home & Garden

God,
My first look in the
bathroom mirror this morning
tells too much truth.
Help me to age gracefully.
Help me to accept getting older
and to relax into this body
you've given me.
Amen

The Bathroom

Home & Garden

God,
There's so much junk in here.
It reminds me
how needlessly complicated
my life can be.
Help me to discern
what I really need
to live well and to let go
of all the rest.
Amen

The Basement and Attic

Home & Garden

God,

I come here

to look at the memories.

My life is rich and full.

Here, I am reminded

of your goodness toward me.

Thank you.

Amen

The Basement and Attic

Short Prayers for Busy Women

Earth & Sky

Earth & Sky

God,
Today is just gorgeous!
The sky is beautiful;
the air is so fresh that
words fail me.
All praise to you,
my Creator!
Amen

Weather

God,

We need rain.

Gardens and crops are bone dry.

Have mercy on us

and send the rains.

Heal the earth,

your creation.

Amen

God,
Last night's snowfall
is beautiful.
All is quiet, hushed by
the fresh snow.
For winter's beauty,
I offer my thanks.
Amen

Weather

God,

All this rain is driving me crazy.

It's dark all the time.

It wouldn't be so bad if I didn't

have to go out in it—

but I do. O God,

how 'bout a little break?

Please send me a little sunshine.

Amen

Weather

Earth & Sky

God,
I know you are much more
magnificent than the thunder.
But as the thunder claps overhead,
I'm reminded of you
and your greatness,
your power.
And I am grateful that
you love me.
Amen

Weather

Earth & Sky

God,
I like walking with you.
I put one foot in front of the other
and feel the earth solid
beneath my feet.
And I know that
your faithfulness toward me
is as solid as a rock.
Amen

Earth

Earth & Sky

God,
The earth has suffered
so much at human hands.
Help me to do all I can every day,
in my small way,
to preserve the earth's resources
and its beauty.
Use me to heal this
lovely planet.
Amen

Earth

God,

Digging in the earth

is the best therapy I know.

I feel all the tension flow from my

shoulders, down my arms,

and out of my fingertips,

to be buried in the soft, warm soil.

Help this earth, in which I dig, to grow

rich and healthy flowers and plants.

Amen

Earth

Earth & Sky

God,

Your voice is

the sound of the sea.

As I listen to the crash of the waves,

help me to hear you

with my heart,

mind, and soul.

Amen

Sea

Earth & Sky

God,

The sea is so vast

and I am so small.

Don't overlook me here

on the shore.

Help me to live courageously

and to love well.

Amen

Sea

Short Prayers for Busy Women

Milestones

God,

Thank you for this life

who is such a gift to others.

Bless this special day;

may it be filled with joy and

delightful surprises.

Amen

Milestones

God,
You know how I love
my dear friend.
Defend her from all harm and sadness
on this, her birthday.
May she know many more,
each filled with
much love and good things.
Amen

Birthdays

God,

Thank you for

the gift of this child.

Send your blessings of love,

health, and happiness

on this birthday and

all the birthdays to come.

And help me to survive

the birthday party.

Amen

God,

It's that time of year.

There's too much to do

and I'm already tired.

As I prepare for the holidays,

help me to slow down

and remember you

and how much you love me.

Amen

Milestones

God,
This is my favorite time of year.
All the lights tell me
that your Light has come
into the world to live among us.
And I rejoice to give you
thanks and praise.
Amen

Holidays

God,

Sometimes there doesn't seem to be

enough of anything during the holidays—

not enough gifts or food or

happiness or love.

Everybody seems to want

more and more. Give to me the peace

of knowing that your love is infinite and

that you are enough for me.

Amen

God,

In spite of all

the people around me,

I am lonely this holiday season.

May I have the honor of your company

and warm myself in the fire

of your love?

Have mercy upon me, O Lord.

Amen

Milestones

God,
The hustle and bustle
of the holidays make me feel so good.
I love the energy and
sense of great expectation.
Help me to slow down
so I don't miss a minute of it—
and so I don't miss the
touch of your grace.
Amen

God,

During this quiet moment

in the holiday season,

let me hear you whisper my name.

Let me know that

your great love for humanity includes

your particular love for me.

In silence,

O God, I offer up my love.

Amen

Milestones

God,
May the joy that these
two wonderful people experience
today strengthen and bind
them together as they journey
into the future.
Let your hand rest upon them
this day–and every day
of their life together.
Amen

God,

Only yesterday, he was a baby.

Now he's getting married.

Watch over and

take care of my baby.

He will need

your love and care for the

long journey ahead.

Amen

Milestones

God,

Sometimes I didn't think

we were going to make it.

But by your grace and

with your help, we did.

Thank you for this marriage.

Today let us each see you

in the other's eyes.

Amen

God,

Through good times

and hard times your hand has

been upon the marriage of these

two beautiful people.

Warm them

with memories of the past

and journey with them

into the future.

Amen

Milestones

God,
Bless our marriage.
Smile on us and let us feel
the warmth of your love.
Give me the courage
to love my partner
even more than I do today.
Amen

Milestones

God,

On this anniversary
of my divorce,
heal any scars that remain.
Help me to let go of
the past so that I may walk
fearlessly into the future.
And let me know that you
walk by my side.
Amen

Divorce

Milestones

God,
Since my divorce
you've been making me
into a new person.
It hasn't been easy.
But I know that my new life
is in your hands and ask that
you do with me
according to your will.
Amen

Divorce

God,
I feel I've just lost a limb.
The divorce is final.
The pain is great;
help me to bear it well.
Amen

Divorce

God,

The divorce is final

and I am free.

Help me to use my new freedom

responsibly and with love.

Journey with me into

a future rich

with possibilities.

Amen.

God,

I'm worried about the kids.

The divorce has hurt them so.

Hide them under

the shadow of your wings.

Help me to love them even more

than I do right now.

Amen

Divorce

Milestones

God,
Make me into a better lover—
physically, emotionally,
and spiritually.
Help me to learn
more about love from you.
And give me the courage to love
fearlessly and truthfully.
Amen

God,

I'm so anxious and worried;

I feel I'm going to explode!

Yet I know that all things rest

in the palm of your hand.

Help me to rest there too,

calmed by your love.

Amen

God,

I'm in love, and

I feel as if I could kiss

the whole world.

Thank you for

the way I feel today.

Help me to stay in love,

and let me rejoice in you,

the Lover of my soul.

Amen

Feelings and Emotions

Milestones

God,

My heart is broken into

so many pieces that I doubt even you

can put it back together again.

Don't let me give up on you.

Mend my heart, I pray,

so that it is even

stronger than before.

Amen

God,

Deep sadness covers me

and darkness surrounds me.

I can barely get out of bed.

Give me strength.

Rescue me from this sadness;

shine your light into the darkness

and lead me back

into life again.

Amen

God,

Save me from a life of fear.

Give me courage and peace that

comes from knowing

you walk beside me,

even when it feels like

you're far away.

Be a present help to me in

this time of trouble.

Amen

Feelings and Emotions

Milestones

God,

Life is good.

I'm pretty happy right now.

Don't let me take happiness

for granted.

Help me to thank you every day

for this gift of happiness.

Amen

Milestones

God,

You are my joy.

For you are the giver of all good gifts

and the many blessings

you shower on me.

Help me to remember always

that I am joyful

because of you.

Amen

Feelings and Emotions

Milestones

God,
I feel like I've been
kicked in the stomach.
I am breathless with grief.
I am beyond sad; I am numb.
Don't leave me like this, O God.
Breathe your Spirit upon me
and let me live again.
Amen

God,

I'm so angry I can't see straight.

Keep me from doing

something I'll live to regret.

Protect me from myself right now,

and guard me

until I've calmed down.

Amen

Milestones

God,

There is a hole in my life today.

I deeply miss

my loved one.

Bless to me your presence

and let me feel

the touch of your love,

for I am in sore need of you.

Amen

Milestones

God,

Why have you taken

this dear person away from me?

I'm hurt and angry,

and I feel so alone.

Please help me. Do something.

I can't see my loved one, but

let me see you today.

Amen

Milestones

God,

I am so sad.

Let me cling to you today

like a child clings to her mother.

Let me know the power

of your love and

the force of your life.

Amen

Milestones

God,

I am breathless with pain.

You are the God of Life.

In you is light, and

there is no darkness at all.

Help me hold fast

to my faith in spite of my grief.

I love you.

Amen

Short Prayers for Busy Women

My Personal Prayers

My Personal Prayers

My Personal Prayers

My Personal Prayers

_____

_____

_____

_____

_____

_____

_____

_____

_____

_____

My Personal Prayers

My Personal Prayers

My Personal Prayers

_____

_____

_____

_____

_____

_____

_____

_____

_____

My Personal Prayers

_____

_____

_____

_____

_____

_____

_____

_____

_____

_____

_____

My Personal Prayers

My Personal Prayers